Meditations of My Heart

Stories and Poems of Faith and Inspiration

Brenda Jean Payne

AuthorHouse™
1663 Liberty Drive, Suite 200
Bloomington, IN 47403
www.authorhouse.com
Phone: 1-800-839-8640

First published by AuthorHouse 1/12/2009

ISBN: 978-1-4389-0962-2 (sc)

Library of Congress Control Number: 2008911946

Printed in the United States of America
Bloomington, Indiana

This book is printed on acid-free paper.

authorHOUSE®

Kaitlyn Kay O'Connor

I dedicate this book to my niece Kaitlyn. She is the greatest tangible gift my family has ever received and our hearts overflow with love for her. As she grows up, may these stories and poems help reveal to her the character of God and the blessings that come with knowing Him.

Table of Contents

Meditations of My Heart

When it was time for me to consider a title for this book, I looked at the collection of stories and poems as a whole and considered what could possibly express what this body of work encompassed. I saw poems written for friends that expressed my heart in ways I could not express it in mere prose or general conversation. I saw stories that unfolded revelations and epiphanies that the Lord had given to me so I might grow not only as a person but as a Christian. Above all, I saw these writings from deep within myself as something to bring glory to God. I wanted to share His love, His gifts and His blessings with others so that they might ponder these things and also be blessed. All of these things led my mind to Psalm 19:14 which says, "May the words of my mouth and the meditation of my heart be pleasing in your sight, O LORD, my Rock and my Redeemer."[1]

I realized that in this verse I found the common denominator of this combination of poetry and prose: they are all meditations of my heart. These are all writings that have focused my mind and my heart on the workings of God in everyday experiences. You'll read about family, friends, and mere acquaintances who have influenced my life in the name of Christ, often times without any realization of doing so. As I reflect on these memories, I realize they encompass the best of the human condition, the best of what people can do and be in the name of Christ. And if that is true, which I believe it to be, then I pray that Philippians 4:8 would encourage the reader to consider "whatever is true, whatever is noble, whatever is right, whatever is pure, whatever is lovely, whatever is admirable—if anything is excellent or praiseworthy—think about such things."[2] In fact, the New American Standard translation of that same verse says to *dwell* on these things. Dwell. Sounds an awful lot like *meditate* to me.

So, what do we get if we meditate on that which is admirable? Well, I recall from my teenage years a conversation with my mother during which she told me that whenever I encountered someone who possessed a quality I admired or respected I should try to take that same quality and instill it into my own life. This is the same advice that the Apostle Paul gives the early Christians right after he encourages them in Philippians 4:8 to dwell on such things. He continues in verse 9 to add, "Whatever you have learned or received or heard from me, or seen in me—put it into practice. And the God of peace will be with you."[3] This is my desire. For you to recognize in this collection the character of God lived out in the day-to-day lives of my family, my friends, mere acquaintances and, I humbly hope, even myself.

Shannon

Shannon lived just around the corner from my family in a cozy middle class neighborhood in Wisconsin. She was a few years younger than me; and when you are a child, those few years are a vast chasm; so I never knew her very well. In fact, I don't think I ever even knew her last name. Despite that, the memory of Shannon is deeply imbedded in my recollections from childhood.

It was the mid-seventies or so when I first remember seeing Shannon in the neighborhood. She stood out because of how different she was from the rest of us. She was unkempt and messy, and so dirty that her white skin could be considered brown. Her clothes were as filthy as she was; her hair incredibly straggly and at least once filled with lice; her clothes more than one size too small. I didn't like it when Shannon came around. To be truthful, I was a little scared by her filth. She lived around the block just three houses from mine. When we rode our bikes around the block, I was scared to go past her house. It was intimidating to go past this dirty house and messy yard. I was also a little scared her parents might be outside. They were rough-looking characters in my timid opinion as a little girl. Most of all, I was scared that Shannon would be standing there wanting to play with me.

Shannon's parents, although mostly unknown to us children, were quite infamous in the neighborhood. When they wanted Shannon to come home at the end of the day, they would stand on their back step and yell at the top of their lungs, "SHAN-NON!" We all knew that soon Shannon would be making her trek home for the evening and it would be safe to play in the front yard without being bothered by her. We also knew that if she didn't get home post haste, we would be able to hear her mother yell at her quite strongly when she did arrive.

Shannon would often knock on the doors of people in the neighborhood looking for some child with whom to play. How I resented my mother when she would make me go in the yard and talk to or play with Shannon. Couldn't Mother see how "icky" Shannon was? Why would she make me do this? Then one day something happened that brought both shock and revelation to me. I was probably around 9 or 10 years old when I came up from playing in the basement to find my mother standing at the back door, handing Shannon a graham cracker with frosting on it! You need to know this frosting was the thin, glazy kind that my mother would make simply by adding a little milk to some powdered sugar. Certainly no treat I would covet as an adult, but as a little kid that was a big deal in our house. What on earth was she doing? Why would she be giving Shannon a treat and not me, her very own daughter? I was furious inside. After Shannon went away, I asked my mom if I could have a graham cracker with frosting and why had she given Shannon a treat and not me? My mom paused and had a conversation with me about Shannon that I have never forgotten.

"Brenda, I gave Shannon that cracker because she was hungry. She did not eat lunch today and you did."

"But why can't she just go to her own house and eat?"

My mother proceeded to give what Paul Harvey would call "the rest of the story." When school wasn't in session and the weather was decent, Shannon would be sent out of her house in the morning and often was not let back home until supper and/or bed time. Her clothes were too small and her hair was messy because her mommy didn't take the time to make sure Shannon was clean and neat. "You notice how Shannon always walks on her tiptoes?"

Of course I had; it was another one of those "weird" things about Shannon that freaked me out.

"She walks on her tiptoes because she doesn't have shoes that fit. It hurts her feet to walk with shoes that small, but if she tiptoes, then the backs of her heels aren't scraped by the shoes. Brenda, imagine if you were Shannon. What if you never had clean clothes to put on? What if you were never allowed to play in the bathtub and get your hair nice and clean? What if you had to stay outside all day; and I would not let you come home to rest because I didn't want you to bother me? What if you didn't have a sister to play with and spent your days alone outside? What if you didn't get lunch and had to go all afternoon with your tummy hungry?"

"You see, honey," my mother continued, "Shannon needs someone to show her love. Jesus loves Shannon just like He loves you. Jesus would want us to be kind to Shannon and help her however we can. Shannon probably doesn't know how much Jesus loves her and that she can have Jesus in her heart. It is up to us to show her what Jesus is like."

At that moment, the shock from watching my mother award Shannon with treats turned into a revelation of what Shannon's life was like. The one thing that stood out in my child-size brain with its child-like theological understanding was SHANNON NEEDS JESUS. So, with that child-like theology, I decided to rectify that situation as quickly as possible. The next time I saw Shannon she was walking past our house and I was in the front yard. I stopped her and proceeded to tell her that she needed Jesus in her heart. Then, she would go to heaven. (And I thought of how wonderful heaven would be for Shannon compared to how she lived here on earth.) So

I *made* Shannon get on her knees in the front yard and had her repeat after me, just like I had seen and heard the pastors and Sunday School teachers do in church. "Dear Jesus," I said. *"Dear Jesus,"* Shannon repeated, *"Please come into my heart and forgive me of my sins."*

Shannon obliged my young evangelistic efforts and repeated everything I told her to say. My mother recalls watching the scene from the front picture window. As an adult, I find it a little humorous to think I was so driven by my passion for winning souls to Christ that I would actually *command* someone to get on their knees in my front yard. But a child's heart is pure and I simply wanted Shannon to know this loving Jesus as much I knew Him. I wanted her life to be better and I didn't want her to be sad and hurting.

A couple years passed and as a 6th grader I overheard two teachers in the hallway talk as Shannon tiptoed in her tight shoes down the hall. One of the teachers must have had Shannon in her class at that time because the other teacher said, "Here comes your tip-toer." And they both chuckled. I truly don't remember who the teachers were, but I remember the pang that went through my heart when they laughed. I wondered if they realized WHY she was tiptoeing. Did they know what kind of home she came from? Did they know how little her parents seemed to care for her? Did they have any idea what that little "tip-toer" went through when she left the school each day?

Just a few years later, Shannon moved away. A man from our church bought Shannon's house for very little money in order to remodel it and sell it for profit. We all knew the poor condition of the outside, but I remember him telling how absolutely filthy it was inside: cigarette burns in the carpet, blackened walls from smoke and filth, and a stench of smells that permeated everything. Upon hearing it, my heart broke once again for Shannon.

As I have gotten older and observed more children, especially in my role as a public school teacher, I have come to sadly discover how many Shannons are in this world. Children who are neglected or ignored; children who don't know what it is like to have new, clean clothes for school or who come to school so hungry their stomachs hurt. Children who don't have birthday parties or sleepovers because their parents don't dare let others see how they live. Children who don't know the peace and love that only God can provide. I am so glad my mother explained to me about Shannon. Not only did it change how I saw her; but it taught me to have compassion for those who aren't the most popular or most beautiful or most talented. What a gift to pass on to your child – the gift of compassion and a desire to reach out to others and bless them in the name of Jesus.

That was about 30 years ago. After her family moved away, I never saw Shannon again. I have, however, prayed for her more than once. I pray that she was able to find some happy times as a child. I pray that she has discovered what it means to truly accept Christ as her Savior, and not just because a neighbor girl makes you repeat a prayer. I pray Shannon was able to overcome what may have been a lifetime of hurt or loneliness. I pray she knows my Savior. I know He loves her and all the other Shannons in the world. Look around your neighborhood. Is there a Shannon to whom you could offer a helping hand? You may be the only link to Jesus your Shannon ever encounters.

"Whatever you did for the least of these...you did for Me."[4]

Musings of a Child

Even as a child I enjoyed writing, especially fiction. I loved when the teacher would assign us the task of creating our own story. Just recently I came across several stories I had written in elementary school. As I read them over the phone to my mom and my sister, we laughed at the funny parts and marveled at the details and at the directions the plots would often take. It brought to mind how much I enjoyed writing as a child. I also came across some poems I had written in my youth. I decided to include three of them here; one from my elementary school years as a ten year old, one from junior high and one from early high school, in that order.

They are not included because of any great poetic technique displayed in their composition. Rather, they are included as an offering to the Lord. I thank Him for showing me a way to express the deepest feelings of my heart when mere conversation can not accomplish the task. While our interests and talents aren't perfected while we are still young, He can take what we offer Him and bless it and allow it to grow into a lifetime passion. So, please read these childhood poems of mine in that light: an offering to the Lord and a foreshadowing of what He can do in our future if we continue to persevere.

Untitled

The trees are cut
Their leaves will fall
Man will die
But some live on for eternity with God

The bird's wings break
Things are wrecked
Shadows fade
The pages will be torn of a book

The pages of life turn
And some are torn
Which causes death

My pages turn as I go on
To new and better things
But memories of you live on

Faith

Lord, hear me when I pray
Know my needs and wants
Let me have faith
That You'll answer my prayers.

In Your Word, in Hebrews 11:6,
You say, "Without faith
It is impossible to please God."
Lord, let me have faith.

I want so much to please You
Through my praise and worship
Look inside my heart, Lord
You'll see I am sincere.

Let me hold fast my feelings
Of love and dedication
Let me not waver
In the sight of my enemies

Lord, grant me faith
That will lead me through
Life's troubling times
Grant me faith like a mustard seed.

You Were There

For all the times I never cried
For all the times I never tried
For all the secrets I never said
For all the tears I never shed

For all the friends I never had
For all the times I stomped off mad
For all the times I cared not
For all the love I never got

For all the times I felt left out
For all the times I had some doubt
For all the dates I never had
For all the times I felt so bad

When I cried unto You, You were there
What I realized is You really care.
Yes, O Lord, You really care
For all the times…..You were there.

The Prayers of a Righteous Man

One day during a women's prayer meeting for church, one of the ladies in our group started praying for the men in our church who were also husbands. The other women there began to echo her prayers and soon the room was filled with a chorus of cries for their men to be the spiritual leaders in their homes. They wanted men who would lead by example through prayer and reading God's Word. As the group continued to pray for their husbands, I thought of a man I once knew named Herb Pharr.

I knew Mr. Pharr because his daughter Janet and I were dear friends growing up in the same church as teenagers. We had many sleepovers at each other's houses with much time invested in the usual topic of conversation for teenage girls; that being "boys." I always enjoyed going to Janet's house because she had a huge bedroom that was far enough away from her parents' room as to prevent most of our giggles and goofy behavior from being a bother to her parents. Our slumber parties, like that of most other young people, involved staying up very late and then, in turn, sleeping late the next morning. This was typically true except for Sunday mornings when we would wake up plenty early to get ready for church. One particular Sunday morning I was walking down her long hallway in order to shower and "beautify" myself for church when I hear a man's voice talking rather fervently. I could not make out what he was saying; but two things were clear. It was her father's voice and it was coming from the hall closet.

I quickly trotted down the long hallway back to Janet's room and said, "Janet! Your dad is talking to himself in the hall closet! What's going on?" Janet looked at me with a look that said, "DUH!" and replied, "That's his prayer closet. That is where he prays every day." Evidently this was the first time I'd been awake early enough at Janet's house to hear this example of prayer. As a Christian, I was very familiar with the concept of having a private or "secret" place to pray. I just had never actually known anyone whose secret prayer closet was literally IN a closet! Janet continued to explain to me that each day her father would spend considerable time in his prayer closet seeking God.

That was just about twenty five years ago. Since then Janet's beloved parents, Herb and Jessie, have passed on into the glory of God's presence in heaven. Twenty five years - and I can still hear his voice calling out to God in prayer in the early morning. Twenty five years – and the example he set is still a part of my memories. That is the kind of testimony the ladies in my prayer group would love to be able to share about their own husbands. Even more so, it is the kind of testimony we all should desire – not for earthly credit, but for the transforming power that prayer can have in our lives as Christians and in our personal relationship with Christ. It is the example that Mr. Pharr set that was brought to the forefront of my memory that day in prayer. It was a call to action; a reminder to maintain my own prayer life; and it was all inspired by *The Prayers of a Righteous Man*.

Early in the morning
Before the sun has even risen
He tiptoes quietly down the hall
To fulfill his daily mission

He enters into the tiny closet
Known only to God and he
He steadies his mind, his heart, his soul
As he bows on bended knee

"Dear God," he cries out in earnest.
"I lift up my family to You.
I pray that they'll learn to love You so
And to Your Word be true."

"Help me, Dear Savior," his prayer goes on
"To love You more each day.
To be faithful to You in all my steps
As I go along life's way."

His soul wells up with fervent prayers
They come pouring from his heart
He does this each and every morn
It's how each day he starts

He continues to pray in secret
Not for recognition or show
He simply desires to love and praise
The One Who loves him so

For while there is no earthly glory
No trophy, no praise, no award
This quiet place yields a sweet perfume
It is the presence of the Lord

Let us learn from this man's pattern
His daily choice to pray
Let us take the time to seek God's face
Each and every day

For it is in this time of quiet
When His voice we learn to heed
That we'll see His hand begin to move
As He meets our every need

Home Folk

It was a simple question. She never could have anticipated that it would have evoked such a response from me. As a second grade teacher, I was sitting in my classroom when a third grade teacher called to me from her room, "Are you going to Evangel's Homecoming?" I answered, "No, I won't be going; in fact, I haven't been back to Springfield since I graduated. But I will someday…you see, I have family there." At the word "family," my throat choked, my eyes welled with tears and my heart overflowed at the memory of my "family" in Springfield, Missouri. I tried to explain in a few sentences what that family had meant to me, how much they had been used by God to bless my life. Words failed me and I could no longer hold back the emotions. They came pouring out of my heart. My co-worker, as a fellow Evangel graduate, knows well the attraction that Springfield holds to those of us who were blessed to be a part of its collegiate charm. She listened, yet I knew she could not fully comprehend, nor could I fully explain, this torrent of emotions I was experiencing.

It was 1988 when I enrolled at *Evangel College,* now *Evangel University.* I had already completed one year of college in Wisconsin and had not had a happy experience. I longed to find a college that would provide wonderful memories as well as a wonderful education. Several weeks prior to the start of the school year, I had received a letter from Park Crest Assembly of God, inviting all new Evangel students to visit the church. My parents and I checked into a hotel before moving day and decided we would go to Park Crest on our first Sunday in Springfield. Having come from a mega-church of 1500 people, I was pleased with what I deemed the *smallness* of Park Crest, which had a congregation of about 600 people at that time. The senior pastor got up to welcome any visitors and in the course of his welcome, my attention was caught by these exact words, "We're just 'home folk' here." At that moment I knew in my heart that this would be the church for me. I wanted a place where there was a sense of true welcome and family fellowship. I wanted to be a part of these "home folk."

Shortly after the start of the semester, the church had an "Adopt-A-Student" program. College students could be "adopted" by a church family; and in turn, the family would invite them to their house occasionally and build a relationship with these students while they were miles away from home. We all gathered in the church gymnasium and were introduced to the family that had been chosen for us. When they called my name and I stood up, I saw the youngest daughter look up at her mom and say with excitement, "We got a girl!" That began my wonderful relationship with the Stephenson family.

When I met this family of six with two girls and two boys, I had no idea how much they would become woven into my heart. During the course of my time there, I was blessed with countless Sunday dinners and family get-togethers, the freedom to do laundry when I needed, and even portions of vacations spent in their house when I could not afford to travel home. Yet, it was more than that. It was a place where I could be myself; yet hold a special place of honor. I was family, yet I was an honored guest. I was a daughter and a sister, but also someone they desired to bless in the name of the Lord. And bless me they did. But besides all the fun times, there were the wearisome times. The times of stress over final exams, the difficulties that come with trying to find God's will for your life, the heartache of failed relationships; in short, the struggles of becoming an adult. They always encouraged, always lifted me up. They were ready to bless me, yet always honest enough to point me in the right direction should I lose my focus.

When I graduated in 1992, I stayed at their home one last time. The morning I left with my small car packed to the hilt, we stood in their foyer in a circle, holding hands for one last goodbye. The parents prayed for my safety and for God's watchful eye over my life. When we were done praying, I started to speak. I wanted some way to let these people know how much they meant to me. They were not just an adopted family; they had become a part of who I was. I wanted to tell them how each had blessed my life. How the youngest boy had shown me the innocence of a child who loves Jesus. How the older boy had shown such remarkable commitment to Christ at such a young age. I wanted to tell the younger daughter how proud (and even a little envious) I was of her amazing talent for singing. I wanted to let the older daughter know I treasured the times we talked and laughed and simply acted like "sisters." I wanted the father to know how much I admired his quiet leadership in his family, his dedication to hard work to provide for those under his care. Most of all, I wanted the mother to know how very much she blessed my life in countless ways. I wanted her to know that I would never forget the role she played in my life by simply opening up her home.

So, as I opened my mouth to speak, to somehow convey all these thoughts and feelings, I could not get but the first word out of my mouth. I was so overcome with emotion that I truly could not speak. The mother looked at me and simply said, "We know. We know." After several hugs and more goodbyes, I got in my car and drove home.

All of these memories, from the first day I met the Stephenson family to the last day I saw them, flooded through my heart in the seconds that followed that simple question: "Are you going to Homecoming?" My spirit was being bathed with a river of recollections that were so sweet and dear. The same flood of emotions that prevented me years ago from saying my goodbyes was now preventing me from being able to explain to my fellow teacher how precious this family was to me. While circumstances and now health have prevented me from returning to Springfield, I do believe in my heart I will be able to visit them one day. I also rest in knowing that we will all meet again in the kingdom of God.

All four Stephenson children have gotten married and some have children of their own. The parents moved to another town. Our contact now is limited to a Christmas card and an occasional email, but they are still a part of who I am. They will always be a part of my fondest college memories. They will always be…my home folk.

The Perfect Matchmaker

"Oh my word!" Katherine exclaimed as she collapsed with laughter onto the bed in my dorm room. She had just come from a date with Tom (*named changed for purpose of anonymity) and evidently had quite the evening.

"How bad was it?" I asked while trying to control my own laughter.

"Oh, Brenda, where do I begin? I mean, I know I wasn't expecting much. I only like him as a friend and I figured, hey, it's a free meal, but c'mon!" Katherine exhaled in frustration. "First, our big dinner out was at the Taco Bell across the street. If I hadn't kept up the conversation at dinner, we would have eaten in silence. Then," she paused for dramatic effect, "we went to a movie."

"What did you see?" I asked, anticipating something ridiculous simply because Katherine had purposefully paused long enough for me to ask the question.

She looked me straight in the eye and said very slowly, "Teenage Mutant Ninja Turtles!"

"Shut up!" I shouted in that way that really means *you've got to be kidding.* "Are you lying to me?"

"Brenda, I tell you the truth."

"Um…aren't you both over twenty years old?"

"Yes, we are."

"Did you want to see that movie?"

"Nope."

"Didn't he ask you what movie you would like to see?"

"Nope."

"So, he just, like, walked up to the counter and bought two tickets for Teenage Mutant Ninja Turtles?"

"Yep."

"So, how was the movie?" I asked, swallowing a smile.

"Exactly what you'd expect: Teenage Mutant Turtles doing their Ninja thing." Both of us looked at each other and burst into laughter simultaneously.

"What did you do," I began after the laughter subsided, "when the movie was over?"

Katherine replied with disinterest, "We came back to campus and that was it." After a thoughtful pause she continued, "Well, at least I obliged him the one date."

That evening had pretty much been the social highlight of Katherine's year. She was graduating that spring and had other things on which to concentrate. When it came time to graduate, Katherine had but one regret over her time at Evangel College. That was simply that nothing more than friendship had ever transpired between her and another student named Don. She had cared deeply for him and it pained her to have him be "the one who got away." But life goes on and Katherine got a job teaching in Illinois for a couple of years. She eventually moved back to her parents' house in Ontario, Canada where she got another job teaching elementary school.

I began to hear about Brian (name changed), an unmarried dentist she had started dating. Soon they were a steady item and Katherine, now in her mid-twenties, had her first real, full-fledged serious boyfriend. But there was one problem in the midst of this fairy tale romance. Katherine, a woman who had spent her entire life loving God and being true to her Savior and His Word, had fallen for a man who not only did not know Christ as his Savior, but had no desire to even go to church with Katherine. The longer Katherine dated him, the more concerned I became. It was so unlike Katherine to not be completely sensible. But she simply wanted what most women want at that age: a good man with a decent job who cares about her romantically. "What's wrong with that?" you might ask yourself. Well, absolutely nothing if the situation glorifies God and is according to His will. After all, 2 Corinthians 6:14 tells us not to be yoked to unbelievers.[5] Our hearts should not be intimately tied to those who do not love our God because then our hearts become torn between allegiance to our Savior and alliance with the world.

Then Katherine became engaged. Actually engaged to be married. My heart was so burdened for I truly believed she was making a mistake. I believed she was settling for this because she didn't want to end up alone and never married. As time went by, I couldn't shake the heaviness in my heart over Katherine's decision. Finally, I realized something: I had to speak up. You need to know a little more about my friend Katherine to understand why I was a little leery about approaching her. She is tall and stately and very self-sufficient. Perhaps time has changed her; but at that time she, like me, was an independent thinker who did not like other people to tell her what to do. She possessed the ability to intimidate with words if a situation warranted it. She took no guff from anyone and wasn't afraid to speak her mind. So, I knew two things for certain. The first is if I truly considered myself a friend who loved her and cared about her and wanted the very best for her life, I must speak up about her decision and encourage her to rethink it. The second thing I believed is that speaking up would end our friendship. She was going to tell me to mind my own business, take care of my own problems and leave her alone. Despite that, I was willing to lose her friendship if it could stop her from making a mistake that she would later regret.

So, I chose a day and a time I knew she would be home and prepared to call her in Canada from my parents' home where I was living in Wisconsin. This was before the days of free cell phone minutes and cheap phone cards, so a long distance call to Canada was not going to be commonplace or inexpensive. I could already picture my father's face opening the phone bill. I had been praying over this whole situation, so before I dialed, I prayed one last time. "Lord, please help me to use the right words to talk to Katherine. I pray she would hear what I have to say and know that I am motivated by love. And, even though I know she will be so angry with me that she will never be friends with me again, I pray she finds a man who loves You first and then learns to love her. May she find the right man who would also be Your will for her life. Help me Lord as I make this phone call now."

Katherine answered the phone and we began to exchange pleasantries like most people do at the beginning of a phone call. "Hi, how are you? What's new?" The whole time my stomach was flip-flopping and my hands were shaking. Finally, I said, "Katherine, there is something I wanted to talk to you about. I'm concerned about your engagement to Brian. You've told me that he does not know Christ as his Savior and that he always finds an excuse not to attend church with you. I know he loves you and is good to you. It must be a great feeling to have a man in your life. But do you really think it's God's will for you to marry him? Why would God choose someone who did not know Him to be your partner forever? Can you really see yourself happily married to someone who does not love the One you love and live for? And if a non-Christian guy can find you attractive and want to marry you, why would you think God could not provide a Christian man who could do the same? I know it's not my life, but as your friend, I needed to tell you that I think you're making a mistake. I really believe God desires more for your life."

There. I'd said what I needed to say. There was silence for a few seconds that seemed to last forever. I held my breath as I waited for her to unleash a tantrum of words on me for sticking my nose into her business. When she did speak, the first words out of her mouth were, "You must really love me to say those things to me." My whole body almost collapsed from the combination of shock and the release of stress. I truly don't recall what else was expressed in that conversation. In fact, I do not think we talked much longer for she had, understandably so, a lot to think about. But that moment in time taught me that anything is possible when it is bathed with prayer. In addition, I learned not to underestimate the value that love and friendship can have in any given circumstance.

I am happy to report that Katherine allowed Brian to fall by the wayside as she moved on with her life. Then some time later, Katherine was on vacation with her parents in another part of Ontario near Niagara Falls. Who does she run into but Don, the One who got away! He was vacationing in the States with his family and they had come across the border by the Falls. During the course of these family vacations, they spent some time together and things progressed from there. Eventually they were married. They now live in Illinois and have two daughters.

Whenever I share Katherine's story with people, I still marvel at the work of the Lord to bring these two people together. A girl from Canada goes to Missouri to attend college. Here she meets a man from Iowa. She moves to Illinois to teach, he gets a job in Washington. She moves back to Canada. While in Canada she travels to another part of the country only to run into Don who had come from Washington back to Iowa to vacation with his family in New York. While it took several years to come to pass, the Perfect Matchmaker brought these two people together whom He had chosen to spend a lifetime as one couple. Two countries, 1 province, and 5 states were traversed in this journey that the two of them made to find each other.

Katherine and Don's amazing journey to find each other should be a testimony of God's ability to arrange our lives exactly according to His will. As long as we submit our lives to His guidance, He makes all things possible. So, do not grow weary at God's timing. His plan and His ways are perfect.

Your wait may seem long; but perhaps it's because your greatest dream of all is being arranged by the One who sees the big picture. When the time is right and the moment is there, your reward, your dream, your answer to prayer could end up being even more incredible than you've ever dreamed.

My parents on their wedding day. April 14, 1963.

Love Predestined
A Tribute to My Parents

While they were yet children
God began to weave their destinies together
He prepared them for the day they would meet
By guiding their lives in the right direction.

Both came from humble backgrounds
So that neither could feel above the other
Both heard of Christ as a child
That salvation might be deeply rooted in their souls.

One experienced great heartache in youth
While the other knew a gentle childhood
Brought together, God provided one whose heart ached
With one who had an understanding spirit

Through the course of time
Each was brought to find the one
Whom God had been preparing
To share a lifetime with the other.

His strength, her grace
His determination, her patience
Predestined by God
To have their souls intertwined…forever.

Kaitlyn – Our Greatest Gift

The Gift

A childless woman weeps from her heart
As she lies face down on her bed
For like after every test in the past
"No baby," the doctor has said

"Why, dear God, why me?" she cries
"I've loved You and called on Your Name
I've prayed and fasted and clung to Your Word.
And yet each result is the same."

Many have prayed for this childless woman
Her husband, her family and friends
The years of waiting seem ever so long
When will the tears and hurt end?

Convinced she has been forgotten
Her heartache goes on for years
Yet while she feels alone and broken
The Lord has been counting her tears

And as she calls out for a baby
Another one learns with surprise
She's carrying a child she can't possibly raise
In hurt desperation she cries

The Lord speaks to the heart of the expecting one
"Give birth to this child and don't fear
For there is one who is waiting in earnest
For a baby to love and hold dear"

So the selfless act of the one with child
Becomes a beautiful gift
As the childless couple readies their home
Their clouds of heartache soon lift.

They now have received the most perfect child
For her eyes, her smile, her face
Are daily reminders from heaven above
Of God's mercy, His love and His grace

They marvel each day at their baby
Their gift - the desire of their heart
The Lord has poured out His blessing
It was His plan from the start

For the Lord knows each child to be born
Each one is special and blessed
He knows to which parents each needs to belong
In each instance He knows what is best

And this couple, now joyous, will never forget
The one who was led by the Lord
To offer in love this child as a gift
And grant them life's greatest reward

So trust the Lord's timing and live in His will
In His wisdom He knows what to do
To answer your prayer and grant you your gift
And show you that dreams can come true.

A Mother's Heart

One morning while my mother was visiting me, she mentioned that one of her dearest friends had called her the previous evening asking for prayer. Her friend had given her permission to share the request with me that I might join with them in prayer. This wonderful Christian lady had told my mother that she recently found out her son was living a life that did not glorify God. He had willingly chosen to turn his back on how he was raised and to ignore the teachings of the Lord he had learned in his youth. We were all shocked at this man's choice; it seemed so contrary to his nature. This mother was beside herself with grief and concern; this was her son, her precious child who was living in a manner that did not lead to the Savior. My heart ached for her.

Later that evening when I began to pray for her son as well as pray for her, my own heart was filled with this overwhelming feeling of grief, a burdensome feeling that I could not pray through to a release. Her heartache had become my heartache; and I could not find the words to adequately pray to God to express the needs of her heart. I kept thinking in my head, "How heavy is this mother's heart." That phrase played over and over in my head as I continued to empathize with this mother and what she was dealing with emotionally and spiritually. Finally, when I thought my own heart would burst, this poem came pouring out and I immediately grabbed paper and pen to record the expressions of my heart. Within a day I had mailed it to her in hopes it might minister to her own heart. It was the only way I could express to her that I understood the burden she was carrying. Perhaps there are other parents who are overcome with grief over their wayward children. I pray this poem will remind them that there is a Savior who cares about the aching in *A Mother's Heart.*

How heavy is a mother's heart
To know her child's sin
How deep the wound, filled with grief,
That flows from her soul within

She cannot force her precious child
To turn to the Savior dear
She can only cry out to Jesus Christ
As she sheds tear after tear

How heavy is our Savior's heart
To know each child's sin
How deep the wounds that pierced His side
And flowed from His soul within

The Savior knows the mother's ache
He feels her burdens true
He'll hold her in His precious hand
And her wayward child, too

While the mother's heart is heavy
To know her child's sin
She knows the Savior's listening
She knows it deep within

So she lays her precious child
Down at the feet of God
And trusts Him to watch her little one
Wherever he may trod

And the mother's heart is hopeful
For the great and glorious day
When her prodigal child declares
The Savior's washed his sins away

In the meantime, she is faithful
Each prayer her Savior hears
And as she cries out, "Dear Jesus"
He will wipe away her tears.

A New Beginning

It was the night before the water baptism of a friend of mine. I knew the next morning I would be driving out of town to visit the church of this co-worker, but I could not fall asleep. She had recently made her heart right with God after many years of not living for His glory. I had been blessed in this circumstance to have prayed for her and encouraged her along this journey. She had now made the decision to follow the Lord's precept in **Acts 2:38** which says, "Repent and be baptized, every one of you, in the name of Jesus Christ...."[6] I told her I would be there to celebrate the day with her. As I lay in bed thinking about the wondrous experience the next day held for her, I wanted to do something more than just give her the gift I'd already gotten her in honor of the day. I wanted to write her a note to somehow convey the feelings of my heart for this moment in her life. However, I could not organize my thoughts to do it justice.

Then, in a flash, a poem began to form in my mind. It was late and I was already tucked into bed with no paper close by; although I did have a pen. I looked over and saw the empty Kleenex box next to the bed and ripped it open to lay flat. I then composed the entire poem rather quickly on the inside of that tissue box. In an instant that tissue box went from being my trash to being a treasure. What a great metaphor for the salvation experience which my friend has just encountered! Our lives are virtually worthless until we allow the great Author of our faith [Hebrews 12:2][7] to put His hand upon us and transform us into His treasure. His treasure – made possible by the forgiveness and healing that His shed blood provides.

The next day I gave my friend a copy of this poem after her baptism. I've included it here so that you might know the glory of a new beginning with God should you need it. May the Lord provide you with a friend who will help you along that journey. However, do not forget to lean on the greatest Friend of all – the great Author and Perfecter of our faith. Only He can truly offer you *A New Beginning*.

When you bow before the Savior
And you ask Him in your heart,
He washes all the old away
And gives you a new start.

Cling to your Savior, dear friend
For He longs to be the One
To complete the work in your life
That He has just begun.

The Christian road may not be easy
And our valleys may be deep,
But the peace and strength He offers
Are always ours to keep.

If you need a friend to lean on
To help you focus on The Way
I'll be there to answer questions
And pray for you each day.

I'll pray that you'll draw closer
To the One who sets you free
And He'll bless you more & more each day
And throughout eternity.

In Your Time of Need
~~for my friend~~

If there are times when you are burdened
By the cares and woes of earth
If you're broken in your spirit
And your soul needs a rebirth

If there are times when you are needy
And seek a miracle or two
If the pain inside is ever great
And you don't know what to do

Lean on me; I'll seek the Lord
I'll lift you up in prayer
I'll take your burdens on myself
Your load I'll help to bear

Just know the Savior loves you
And wants to meet your needs
He longs for you to know His voice
To follow where He leads

So while you wait for answered prayer
And relief from all your woes
May you give your heart to Jesus
And see how your faith grows

Faith to trust the Savior
Who hears each prayer request
He'll take your hand and draw you near
And forever you'll be blessed

The Howell family homestead. To the left is the chicken house, to the back and right are the outhouse and the cow barn.

Life in a Small Town

I have never encountered anyone with more fondness for her hometown than my own mother. In my childhood we visited Wilmot, South Dakota, a small community of approximately six hundred people, about once a year. The home of my grandparents was a wonderful place to behold. From the crab apple trees in the south to the forest of trees to the north, Grandpa and Grandma Howell had the biggest "yard" I've ever seen in my whole life. My grandparents' farm was a magical place filled with more wonders than a city girl could ever imagine. There was a hen house where my sister and I were actually allowed to search the nests and the loose hay for newly deposited eggs. There was the feed building that contained, in addition to animal feed, stale corn cobs stored for a variety of uses. The cow barn, as well as the pig barn, contained many odors to which I never did adjust, but for my mother still remain the sweet perfume of her childhood.

It was on this farm where I learned the hard way what a "cow pie" was. It was on this farm where I learned how and felt privileged to use an old-fashioned water pump behind the farm house. It was there I saw an outhouse for the very first time; the same outhouse that served as Grandpa's private sanctuary for their tenure on the farm. And it was on this farm that I saw death for the first time. A sow was giving birth and Grandpa was standing watch. Just a little girl at the time, I stood in awe as the mama pig instinctively knew how to birth her own babies and clean them off post-birth. It was appalling and, at the same time, a mind-boggling event to behold. However, one of these baby pigs came out looking differently from the rest. I can still see a little pig whose color was markedly darker than the others, almost a deep purple. I remember looking at my mother who was standing next to me and asking why that pig was different. As Grandpa took that pig away, mom explained to me that the baby pig was stillborn. My little heart was crushed. I remember running out of the barn and crying so hard. I especially remember praying for God to bring that baby pig back to life. But after a later return to the pig barn, I discovered that my prayer had not come to pass. My heart ached for days over the loss of that pig. It is the only sad memory I have of my time spent on my grandparents' farm.

As interesting as the outside farm activities with Grandpa were, the inside activities with Grandma were just as delightful. I have come to believe that my cooking and baking skills are a direct result of the skills passed down from my Grandmother to my mother to me. Grandma created such wonders that my own mother, while capable, often didn't take the time to bake. Cakes, date cookies, and the treat to top all treats – divinity candy! It wasn't just the sweets that were delicious. Every meal was a composition of delectable foods, even the bacon and eggs for breakfast had a flavor that seemed to rise above the ordinary. Often my sister and I would awake and be ready for breakfast as Grandpa was coming inside for his morning coffee break, having had his breakfast hours earlier. So in addition to the bacon and eggs, there was the smell of fresh coffee and a plate of cookies on the table of which Grandpa and ultimately the two of us would partake. Cookies for breakfast?! Only at Grandma's!

The smells and sounds of the farm are as much a part of my memories as the sights and activities of my time spent there. Whenever I hear morning doves "coo" at each other, I am immediately transported to the pull-out couch in my grandparents' living room where I lay on a cool summer morning. The sound of crickets chirping brings to mind an evening concert of sound heard on my grandparents' front porch as the crickets let us all know they were not to be forgotten in the menagerie of the farm. Whenever I smell coffee brewing along with bacon and eggs frying, I see myself as a young child in the quaint kitchen of my grandmother. In addition, let me not forget to mention the beautiful smell of newly mown hay coupled with the stench of fresh cow pies that bring to mind the mysteries of nature that surrounded that farm in Wilmot.

I also recall with great fondness the relaxed pace at which everyone in Wilmot seemed to operate. Evenings were spent chatting or playing cards. Sometimes visitors would stop in and Grandma would serve a "lunch" of coffee and miscellaneous treats. People seemed interested in being friendly and helpful toward their neighbors with a genuine interest in knowing them personally. When driving into town from the farm, Grandpa would wave at everyone from the driver's seat in his pick-up truck, whether he knew them or not.

In my memories, Wilmot will always hold that special quality of yesteryear. It is a nostalgic sweetness that can only be associated with the pleasant memory of times gone by. My mother holds her childhood recollections of this special place in even higher regard than I. She can tell stories about attending the one room school house just up the road from their home. She recalls with great laughter and fondness the use of their party-line phone. I've heard tales of Saturday night on Main Street in this little town of Wilmot. Mother even remembers with gentle affection being able to determine that the family was going visiting - simply by noticing if her mother put on lipstick in the evening after supper dishes had been cleared away; and the kitchen was clean.

My Grandpa doing chores as a young boy, circa 1922. This is the same land he farmed as an adult and where he and Grandma raised their three children.

Grandma allowed my sister and I to help her in the kitchen
as she made her delicious homemade buns. 1973.

I imagine the small size of Wilmot makes a lot of its down-home, welcome-to-all atmosphere possible, but I think the people must have a great deal to do with it as well. Small town folk seem more apt to help others, to step up in difficult times and be a true neighbor to those around them. Such was the case in 1954. It was late January when Alice Eastman decided she was sick and tired of her freezer taking up so much room in their pantry. She decided she could conserve space by placing it flush up against the back staircase. "After all," Alice said to her husband Howard, "we hardly ever use that staircase anymore – it's always the front stairs. Please move this out of the way and then I can have more room to move around in that pantry." Howard probably muttered the obligatory spousal response, "Yes, dear" but went about his business of tending to the immediate chores that held priority.

A couple days later, Howard and Alice went to a dance in a nearby town. They knew they would be getting home very late, so they left their high school daughter in charge of the other four girls. Quite sometime after midnight, one of the girls awoke to discover smoke filling the house. Her fearful heart realized, "FIRE!" The entire front staircase was filled with fire and smoke. The girls upstairs had to get out – the only way was down the back staircase! The girls all escaped the burning house and stood away from the house as they watched their home burn.

The party-line phone at the home of Francis and Lorene Howell rang sometime after 2 a.m. In 1954, a phone call in the middle of the night was never ignored, but answered immediately for it was the sign of something serious. My Grandpa heard someone talking on the party line calling people for help – the Eastman home was on fire! In an instant, Grandpa had on his bib overalls and was on his way to the Eastman's – just one home north and to the west of his. My grandfather, along with several other men, entered that fiery furnace to pull out as many possessions and bits of furniture as they could before the severity of the flames overtook that structure. There likely wouldn't have been any homeowners insurance or replacement cost coverage back then. These men were putting themselves in harm's way to help salvage as much as they could for the neighbors who were still not home from the dance.

Someone suggested the girls, especially the little ones, be taken to neighboring houses for safety. You see, on February 2, 1954, in Wilmot, South Dakota, it was close to zero degrees Fahrenheit after midnight. It was literally freezing cold as those five girls stood in their pajamas on the lawn. According to the story as it has been told and retold over time, a couple of the younger girls went to neighbors' homes for warmth and safety. This included Janet, the 9 year old, who went to Grandpa and Grandma's house, for my mother and Janet were good friends. Meanwhile, on the lonesome highway in the dark of the night, Alice Eastman probably leaned against her husband's shoulder on their late drive home. "I had such a nice time tonight dear; thank you so much for taking me to the dance. It was a nice change of pace during a cold and dreary winter."

"You're welcome," he responded. "And, I'm sorry for not getting that freezer moved for you yet. I'll get it done soon." The Eastmans continue to make small talk as Alice's eyes start to flutter with the heaviness of sleep. As they near home, she hears a strange tone in her husband's voice as he says, "ALICE!" As they get closer and closer to their homestead, they see the billowing smoke and know that something is on fire. As they turn the corner on the dirt road they see their home completely engulfed in flames. Panic fills their entire bodies as they see their neighbors pulling wreckage from their house. Quickly their eyes scan the crowd for their children, their five precious girls. Alice begins to cry uncontrollably and Howard is weak at the knees as they both realize that only some of the girls are standing off to the side. Where were the others? They were nowhere to be seen. In their hearts they believed this could only mean one thing: this inferno had devoured some of their truly priceless possessions. Unable to even process this tragedy, they get out of their car as neighbors begin to surround them. Quickly someone explains that the younger girls were all sent to safety rather than have them stand in the cold. Immediately a wave of relief that cannot be equaled by any other joy flooded their souls. Everyone was okay!

As time passed, the Eastmans rebuilt their house and it was once again their home and their haven. I'm sure many were the times that Alice and Howard both thanked God for His mercy and protection. I'm sure they were both grateful that the freezer which had just a few days earlier been a nuisance, had not yet been moved to block that staircase. That back staircase: the only way of escape for their children. What a blessing that second staircase had been! For even though on that cold winter's night in 1954, the Eastman's lost a great deal of what they owned, the Lord provided a way to save the most important thing in their home: their family.

As I reflect on this story, I marvel at several things. I stand amazed at the providential timing of NOT moving a freezer. Be assured that it was no coincidence; that was the Lord's merciful timing. And even though I never knew Alice and Howard, I can feel in my heart the incredible joy that would replace the overpowering grief when they realized their girls were safe and not lost in the blaze. I stand in awe to hear of men willing to leave their homes in the middle of a very cold winter's night and risk their own lives to help a neighbor save what little they could from that fire. I'm sure Wilmot is not the only place where there are people whose character would incite them to selfless action. Yet, I believe it's the kind of neighborly love that is best fostered in a small town.

Life in a small town cannot be fully appreciated or understood by those who have never experienced it. It is the kind of place that can throw a parade and all the spectators know all the participants. It is the kind of place that can offer a dinner event to the whole town and have it take place in the local high school gymnasium. It's true that life in a small town results in most everyone knowing everything about everyone. But it also means your neighbors know when you need help, encouragement or even a kind word. It is all these things and so much more than cannot be fully explained in words. Life in a small town has a spirit that defies description, yet allows it to remain the lifeblood of its residents; even decades after they have moved away. Perhaps that is why my memories of Wilmot are so dear and why my mother's heart will always guide her home.

Grandma Payne, circa 1985.

Living a Legacy

My Grandma Payne spent the last 19 years of her life as a widow. While my dad would fly across the country to visit his mother every year, it was too expensive for the whole family to fly very often and way too far to drive. However, we kept in touch through letters and phone calls and our occasional visits. Grandma spent the majority of her time reading and studying the Bible as well as praying. Because she seemed to be enveloped in the Lord's presence, I stood in admiration of her single-mindedness for God. In fact, I always viewed her as the spiritual matriarch of our family.

I've felt a call on my heart to be used in ministry since I was a child. I think because of that, I felt a connection to Grandma's role of spiritual leadership since I was very young. After Grandma was diagnosed with cancer and given a short time to live, I began to feel or believe that somehow her passing into heaven's gates would mean a passing of a spiritual mantle to me. I had read a book around this time that involved a son receiving a spiritual "mantle" from his father and as a result, he received his father's spiritual talents and gifts. Having a tendency toward the dramatic, I envisioned myself as the recipient of a great spiritual event, with God's power physically descending on me at the very moment my Grandmother entered into His presence. So as her numbered days began to dwindle, I began to listen for a special voice and watch for a supernatural event that I was sure was going to occur. On April 19, 1995, my mother called me after work to say that Grandma Payne had passed away.

"Really?" I thought to myself. Where were the heavenly lights, the burning bush or the pillar of fire? Where was the great spiritual event that was to be bestowed upon me as a spiritual legacy from my Grandma? There was nothing but simple peace. While I usually try to remain ever hopeful in all things, I must admit I was disappointed. I felt like Grandma had something special when it came to God and I wanted that special connection as well. However, life went on as normal and my father stayed out West to help settle things with Grandma's estate. Weeks later, my mom, my sister and I drove to the airport to pick him up with plans that we would stop at my apartment on the way home for the homemade pie and coffee that I had waiting for everyone.

As Dad was putting his luggage in the car at the airport, he handed my sister and I each some papers and letters that Grandma had saved from us over the years. On one envelope of a letter I had once mailed her, I saw her handwriting and immediately thought, "Aha! This is it! Somewhere in these letters Grandma has written something; something for me to discover after her passing; some great spiritual truth that she intended to pass on to me. (Like I said, I tended toward the dramatic.) As we drove home, I carefully read through each and every card my dad had handed me. It became increasingly difficult to read in the car as the sun began to set. The notes in Grandma's handwriting that I had noticed had so far turned out to be nothing more than grocery lists or miscellaneous notes to herself that she had scribbled on the backs of envelopes. Still, I continued to search, positive I was going to find some life-changing spiritual revelation. Finally, I saw on one envelope a scripture reference with chapter and verse. I did not know the verse just from the reference, but I felt my heart begin to beat faster with the anticipation of being able to look up the verse as soon as I got home. Surely this was it.

We got to my apartment and as my family went into the living room to sit down, I snuck into my extra sitting room to look up the scripture Grandma had written on that envelope. This could be the moment for which I had been hoping and waiting. All the air came out of my lungs as I sighed in disappointment. It was no "special" verse. It was an ordinary, every day Bible verse that did not seem to hold any great spiritual revelation. I was so disappointed. Not just because I didn't get a fanfare experience of God's anointed blessing, but also because it made me question the special spiritual connection I'd always felt I had with Grandma Payne. I went into the living room to serve my family the pie and coffee. After a time to "catch up" with Dad, everyone left. My heart still felt deflated from earlier in the evening. Then I thought, "Maybe I was wrong; maybe in my haste and excitement I looked up the wrong verse. Yes! That must be it. Let me go get my Bible again."

So, I carefully and painstakingly looked up the verse, checking and double checking to make sure I was in the right spot. Sure enough, it was the same verse. The same ordinary verse. I began to pray: "Lord, You know I'm disappointed. You know I was hoping for one last spiritual truth or blessing from Grandma meant just for me. You know my heart is a little discouraged right now; please help me." Then my mind and heart began to wonder, "What if that ordinary, everyday verse is the legacy that God wants me to inherit?" For you see, the scripture reference written in Grandma's handwriting was Matthew 7:12 which states, "Therefore, treat people the same way you want them to treat you."[8] Hmm…the golden rule: *Do unto others as you would have them do unto you.* There is no great mystery hidden in that verse from Matthew. It is as simple and straightforward as a verse can get.

It is so straightforward that people in the secular world quote it all the time and most of them probably have no idea it is from the Bible. In fact, a couple of years ago the school where I was teaching second grade was instituting a new character education program in hopes of enhancing student cooperation and improving behavior. The program, available to public schools nationwide, came with posters containing catch phrases of the main themes of the program. We had posters all over school in big bold print that said, "TREAT OTHERS LIKE YOU WANT TO BE TREATED." Every time I went past one of those posters I would laugh inside. Despite all the efforts in today's society to keep the name of God or His principles out of our public arena, God's Word was literally hanging all over the walls of our public schools and no one, including district administrators, seemed to have a problem with it. Our principal even quoted the posters over the intercom on a regular basis. So be aware fellow Christians: God will allow His Word and His truth to break through even the greatest of blockades.

However, my revelation of Matthew 7:12 was ten years before these school posters came to be. As I sat on the couch in my apartment, I thought over this verse. In reality, this "simple" verse *could* be life-changing. What if we always treated others like we desire to be treated? What if we earned the reputation of one who, while not famous or flamboyant, rich or charismatic, was able to *live* a legacy of kindness? You see, in order to *leave* a legacy, you must first *live* it out in the day to day. What if you could be known as the person who was patient to a fault and forgiving of all offenses? What if we truly lived the way Christ wanted us to live? What if, with every breath we take, we are living testimonies to the character of our Savior?

We could become the kind of people who are unwearied and uncomplaining in long lines and kind to the minimum wage worker who might fail to meet the mark of employment excellence. We would pay our debts and our taxes on time or work hard at our jobs until we could afford to recompense what we owe. We would speak kindly of others and help our neighbors whether they've helped us or not. We would forgive our family, our friends and even strangers as easily as Christ forgives us our wrongdoings. We would err on the side of mercy and generosity even to those who might not fully deserve it. In short, we would live out a legacy that would draw people to Christ, a legacy that reflects God's best and not our worst. Imagine what could happen for God's glory if we truly took hold of that verse. We could transform our homes, our neighborhoods, and our places of work. It is possible for it to ripple even further from there.

So, the next time your day has exhausted your patience and you want to snap at your co-worker or even your spouse, rethink your heart's motivation. The next time a neighbor you aren't friends with needs some help, be the first to step up. Think about the *most* you can give others, not the least. I believe my Grandma would take joy in knowing her life and even her death encouraged me to live such a life…not for her glory, but to bring glory to our God. Start today; a new beginning to your own personal legacy for those you love. It is the legacy I hope to live out each day. It is the legacy I hope to leave behind.

For My Dearest Friend

Dear Friend,

Not too long ago a college professor who was suffering from a terminal illness became well-known to the general public for something he entitled, "The Last Lecture." It was a lecture he gave and later published in book form that he intended to leave behind as his final thoughts of wisdom and insight, particularly for his wife and child. This caused me to ponder what I might say to those I love if I knew it might be the last conversation I would ever have with them. Too often, we put off saying things that might seem over-emotional or too personal – whether out of fear or embarrassment or simple laziness. So, while I have no plans or desire to leave this earth for a few decades, I'd like to share with you my heart in a way that I perhaps have failed to do as of yet.

First I need to say how much I love you. "Love" might seem an awkward word for platonic friends, but I truly do love you. I consider myself so fortunate for having you in my life. In the course of all the times we've spent together, I treasure every gale of laughter, every secret, every encouragement and every heartache that we have shared. When you would tell me things in confidence to keep as private, I felt so honored that you trusted me. When you gave me compliments, no matter how little or casual, I felt special and important. When you helped me with tasks that were beyond my capabilities, I felt incredibly blessed. We don't always express our feelings of gratitude for day to day occurrences, but I would like to do that now. So, for all these things and so much more, dear friend, I humbly and gratefully thank you.

And yet mere gratitude doesn't seem like enough. It fails to repay the debt of friendship I have incurred in knowing you. I realize I could never fully repay your deeds of kindness and expressions of charity during times I was too discouraged or weary to help myself. As I considered this for a moment, I suddenly recalled a short poem I learned even before I was in Kindergarten. I was assigned a portion of it to recite in a Christmas pageant. I believe it went like this:

> *What can I give Him, poor as I am?*
> *If I were a shepherd, I'd give Him a lamb.*
> *If I were a wise man, I'd do my part*
> *What can I give Him – I'll give Him my heart.*[9]

And it occurred to me that my heart is all I can possibly give you. My heart overflows with a love that I hope you also have. It is a love for the Savior of the world. This Savior, of course, is Jesus. I want you to know Him as I know Him: my Forgiver, my Healer, my Redeemer, my Comfort, my Joy, my Hope, my Eternity, my All-in-All.

He's not just a man who lived long ago, but He's the risen Savior who was literally tortured to death just that I might find forgiveness and eternal life. However, it wasn't just for me; it was for you, too. He loves you more intimately and completely than any other created thing could love you. It's His desire for you to know Him and love Him because He knows what a difference it would make in your life. But He wants your whole heart, not just a portion; not just a Sunday heart, but a Monday through Saturday heart as well. He wants you to love Him completely so that He can bless you overwhelmingly. He wants to be the center of your very being.

When I think of how much of our hearts we give to the Lord, I realize that anything less than everything is simply not enough. I know I am much happier and more at peace when I am closer to God's heart rather than when I am further away. It is the times I am frustrated or discouraged or empty when I realize I need more of Jesus: more time praying, more time reading His word. When I make that decision to draw closer to God and live like He lived, suddenly my heart soars with such joy and freedom; I wonder how I can ever be lax in loving Him. That love overflows to you, my friend. I am overwhelmed with a desire for you to feel that same joy, that same freedom, that same forgiveness, that same hope and that same salvation. It only comes when Jesus is the Savior of your heart.

And that is the essence of *my* heart, dear friend. It is all I have to give you: the living testimony and life experience of loving the Savior of the world. What He can give you is so much greater, for only He can give you forgiveness and eternal life. What can you give Him in return? It's simple. Your heart.

With all that I am and ever hope to be,

Brenda

Endnotes

[1] **The NIV Study Bible**. Zondervan Bible Publishers. Grand Rapids, Michigan. 1985.

[2] **The NIV Study Bible**. Zondervan Bible Publishers. Grand Rapids, Michigan. 1985.

[3] **The NIV Study Bible**. Zondervan Bible Publishers. Grand Rapids, Michigan. 1985.

[4] **The NIV Study Bible**. Zondervan Bible Publishers. Grand Rapids, Michigan. 1985. Matthew 25:40.

[5] **The NIV Study Bible**. Zondervan Bible Publishers. Grand Rapids, Michigan. 1985.

[6] **The NIV Study Bible**. Zondervan Bible Publishers. Grand Rapids, Michigan. 1985.

[7] **The NIV Study Bible**. Zondervan Bible Publishers. Grand Rapids, Michigan. 1985.

[8] **The New American Standard Bible**. Copyright © 1960, 1962, 1963, 1968, 1971, 1972, 1973, 1975, 1977, 1995 by The Lockman Foundation Used by permission. (www.Lockman.org)

[9] **Precious Moments Insert**. Precious Moments, Inc. Licensee Enesco Corporation. Hong Kong. 1995.

About the Author

Brenda Jean Payne has been a public school teacher for 15 years in Illinois. She received her Bachelor's degree in Music Education from Evangel University in Springfield, Missouri and her Master's degree in Education from National Louis University in Evanston, Illinois. In addition to serving as music director in various churches and a speaker at church conferences and retreats, she has taught numerous Bible Studies and Fellowship groups for women and hosted several prayer groups as well. She lives close to her family in Kenosha, Wisconsin.

For more information contact shelterministries@wi.rr.com